PROLOGUE
The Garden of Eros

PROLOGUE

THE GARDEN OF EROS

See, in a glade of green moss, watered by a spring, a merry company languidly playing. Flutes, and harps, and panpipes are there; and on wonderful chased silver, figured with the loves of the gods, are cups of beaded wine, and fruits, and honey, and cakes of divers sort. It is night, but the moon is exceeding bright; and the stars shine in the self-luminous blue of the vault. Around the glade are many trees; the ground is a mass of flowers, and gathered roses cover the white limbs of many of the players. One girl is standing, and a full nightingale song trills from her ivory throst. Upon a tall tree of massy foliage sits, hidden from the players, a vulture vast and vague in his black night of shadow. His face is human, of the ovine type, as that of a low-class Jew. He watches the scene throughout in silence, but with intense envy disguised as disgust.

DORIS

Praise the wine wittily!
Praise the wine well!
Footing it prettily
Down through the dell.

Are there not playmates
    Enough and to spare,
Gallant and gay mates,
    Each one of us fair?

Bountiful measures of
    Beautiful wine:
Infinite treasures of
    Bacchus divine!
Hail to the Lord of us!
    Blithe is his reign.
Be thou adored of us,
    Soul without stain!

Fair are the faces, and
    Limbs of us light,
Tracing the paces, and
    Drunk with delight.
Io! let us tremble in
    Trance of the tune
Here that assemble in
    Joyaunce of June!

ATTHIS

Doris, our darling! How subtle and sweet
The throb of thy throat to the flit of our feet!
Come, I have chosen thee.

DORIS

                                Follow me then
Deep in the dance to the heart of the glen!

MARSYAS

Ho! you are rich, you are red, you are ripe!
Pace me your passions to plaint of my pipe!

OLYMPAS

Nay, I am with thee, my master, to match
Every my song to thy lyrical catch.

EROTION

Nay, let us follow you - all in a ring!
Wonder of wisdom and wit on the wing!

ANAXIMANDER

Come, my Giton, of the hyacinth hair!
Apollo, Apollo! indeed they are fair!

HYLAS

Kiss me again, my Lysander, my love!
Listen! Olympas is singing above.

LYSANDER

Ah! but Erotion beckons me yonder!
Beautiful curls on her bosom that wander
Tempt me to folly.

HYLAS

                                             Indeed, let us press
The exquisite doubt in a certain Lysander

LYSANDER

Even as the feet of the maid on the grapes
Crush the wine of delight from ambiguous shapes!

OLYMPAS

Shrill, shrill the never-cloying
 Thirst of maid's enthusiasm!
Atthis with her Doris toying
 In the moonlight filled with laughter,
 Wrestling, kissing - follow after
 To the summit of the spasm!

CHIRON

Ho, shall we sit idle gazing
On such beauty spirit-crazing?
No, my ladies, I'm the song!

ATTHIS

We can sing you!

DORIS

 Sweet and strong!

ANAXAGORAS

Laughter, laughter! I'm for thee,
Doris of the blue-black tresses!
Mine are musical caresses
Like the murmur of the sea.

HYCINTHOS

Chiron, shall we dance with these
Under the acacia trees?

CHIRON

Yes, if Rhodon there will lend us
Her red fleece - like sunset glowing,
With the doubtful venture showing
Where - what God shall there befriend us?

RHODON

Mocker! I shall come. Beware
Lest my manhood match you there!

SILENUS

Ha, you rogue, if Rhodon rage,
Poets earn a cynic page;
And our lips with laughter curl
If she treat you as a girl.

CHIRON

Brute, get back to wine, and leave us
In our flower-love to inweave us.
All we know the shameless chorus:
"Fie! Silenus - Heliorus!"

HELIORUS

I had better right to mock you,
Graceless Chiron, with the quip

(Girls, come close - the jest will shock you)
"Pine-tree with the drooping tip!"

CHIRON

Oh, you little toad of spite!
Come, and I will set you right.
All you year of wantoness
Shall not save you - much distress.

HELIORUS

Yes - the pain I had before.
"At the game that Chiron shouldn't,
Chiron would - and Chiron couldn't"

RHODON

Never heed the little whore!
Play a melody, Marsyas!

HELIORUS

He's at Anaxagoras!

RHODOPE

Where is Doris, then?

ERRINNA

By Zeus,

Where her ribs are all in use!

ANTINOUS

Sprinkle me with poppy-juice
From the flowers of Syracuse
  On the lips relaxed with pleasure
  Of their kisses overmeasure!

Let them suck the heavenly sleep!
Let me sink into the deep!
  Till the morning pale and fresh
  Find my flesh against his flesh,
And mine eyes within his eyes
Watch the sun of glory rise!

All my breath is like new wine.
I have flaxen hair and fine.
  From my shoulders to my feet
  Like the sunlight in the wheat!
  If I laugh, the moon-curved pearls
Match and master any a girl's.
If I weep, as joy may weep,
  One would say the fountain-steep
Of Dione dropped its dew
Through the vivid veil of blue.

I am limber like a snake.
I am soft, and slow to slake—
  For a curling, crimson fire
  Floods my lips and feeds desire.
I am passionate and pale;
Virile - and most faery frail.

  All diverse delights are mine.
  Kiss within me, and combine
To a languorous lyric lure
Sweet as pleasure, and as sure!

SILENUS

Tut, my lad, you do not mention
Modesty.

ANTINOUS

'Twas mine intention,
But those loose lips wine-corrupt
Always itch to interrupt!

SILENUS

Nay, boy, all the song was true.
Come and frisk it once together!
Ah, the goodly Grecian Weather!
Ah, the heavenly haze of blue,
That must set an azure frame
Round the flaxen locks aflame!

CHRYSIS

Come, Evadne, let us fling
Flowers upon them gambolling!

EVADNE

Chrysis! could one weary of
All thine opulence of love?

CHRYSIS

I am fair; I cannot fear.
Was my tongue too eager, dear?

EVADNE

Never, never, never! Here,
Coil the roses close, a cluster
In the flax, the lyric lustre!

CHRYSIS

In the white waves that carouse
On the satyr's beetle brows,
Plait a wreath of laurustine
With the broad leaves of the vine!

SALMACIS

Sweet Lysander, now thou knowest
All the oracle obscure!

LYSANDER

In my soul - my soul! - thou flowest
Suave and sibylline and sure.
O the stream I launched this boat on!
O the pool my fancies float on!
I am drowned in bays of bliss—
Salmacis! - my Salmacis!

HYACINTHOS

Heliorus, siren!
  I have overmatched thee now;
From the bag of Chiron
  Drawn a luckier lot than thou!

SILENUS

Come, we have dallied long enough
With music and with love.
Set to the wine, and slide.
Each twined like vines, fair boy, fair bride,
Down the long glade of sleep,
At the sun's summoning.
We shall be carolling, upon the steep,
The happy dawn's return.
We shall wake - and bathe - and burn.

EROTION

Now the drowsy Lord unloose
All his store of poppy-juice!
   To the murmurous bell-clear fret
   of the tremulous rivulet
Let us lisp the lullaby
Of Arcady - in Arcady!

Me ye know, the dazzling dream
Of the swimmer in the stream.
   Boy to girl and maid to man,
   Mine are all joys of Pan.
Chrysis seeks the darling dove,
Gets the eagle to her love.
   Hylas, trembling toward the pine,
   Finds the soft voluptuous vine.

RHODOPE

Curl ye close! Curl ye close!
Fold your petals like the rose!
All the satyr's lust of limb;

All the delicate and slim
Slenderness of laughing faun
Twine like serpents on the lawn;

All the boy's undulant grace
To the nymph's fantastic face;
All the maiden's chaste delight
To the flushed hermaphrodite;
While the balanced strength of man
Bears its witness unto Pan.

CHRYSIS

Ah, the purple vein that glows
Through the eyelids as they close!
Hush! the breeze that fans the fern
Bids the midnight moon to turn.
We must sleep
Soft and deep:
We must wake — and bathe — and burn.

(The company being asleep, fallen lax in mid-caress, there
enter a Philosopher Heracleitus and his Disciple Chrysippus.)

HERACLEITUS

Look, my darling, and confess
Life one flame of loveliness!

CHRYSIPPUS

Master! Master! how fairy fond
Is yonder maid like a lily-frond!

Let us lie on the moss by the spring, let us share

In their silence serene, the languor rare!
For oh! my lover, I never did see
So goodly a company.

HERACLEITUS

Wait but a moment - stand apart,
Revolving the light in thine innermost heart!
Content not the soul with the skin of the grape!
But the fume of the juice shall inform its shape
With a truer sense than the eye and the ear
Make to appear!

CHRYSIPPUS

Verily, master, I obey.
I travel the exalted way.
I pierce the sense; I gain the goal,
Distil the essence of the soul—

HERACLEITUS

I shroud thee in the web of wool.
I lift the burden of the bull.
Lion and eagle! dart ye forth
Into the cold clime of the North,

Where past the star that points the pole
Rests the unstirred axis of the soul.

CHRYSIPPUS

Hear then! By Abrasax! the bar
Of the unshifting star
Is broken — Io! Asar!

My spirit is wrapt in the wind of light;
It is whirled away on the wings of night,
Sable-plumed are the wonderful wings,
But the silver of moonlight subtly springs
Into the feathers that flash with the pace
Of our flight to the violate bounds of space.
Time is dropt like a stone from the stars:
Space is a chaos of broken bars:
Being is merged in a furious flood
That rages and hisses and foams in the blood.
See! I am dead! I am passed, I am passed
Out of the sensible world at-last.
I am not. Yet I am, as I never was,
A drop in the sphere of molten glass
Whose radiance changes and shifts and drapes
The infinite soul in finite shapes.
There is light, there is life, there is love, there is sense
Beyond speech, beyond song, beyond evidence.
There is wonder intense, a miraculous sun,
As the many are molten and mixed into one
With the heat of its passion; the one hath invaded
The heights of its soul, and its laughter is braided
With comets whose plumes are the galaxies
Like winds on the night's inaccessible seas.
Oh master! my master! nay, bid me not ride
To the heaven beyond heaven; for I may not abide.
I faint: I am frail: not a mortal may bear
The invisible light, the abundance of air.
I fail: I am sinking: O Thou, be my friend!
Bear me up! Bear me up! Bear me up to the end!
Now! Now! In the heart of the bliss beyond being
The None is involved in the One that, unseeing,
Dashes its infinite splendour to death
Beyond light, beyond love, beyond thought, beyond breath.

Ah! but my master! the death of the sun —
Break, break, the last veil! It is done — It is done,

   (He falls, as one dead, upon the grass.)

HERACLEITUS

I bless these happy virgins, souls unstained,
Through whose delight my darling hath attained

Even to the uttermost silence that may be
Even in this vast circuit of eternity.
So, o my golden charioteer, I creep
Into thine arms, and dream the dream of sleep.

   (He sleeps. Upon the still beauty descends from his tree
the man-vulture.)

THE VULTURE

Yaugh Waugh!
Butch! this is terrible
That all these people should be happy — Pss! —
Without a thought of Me!
Ga! Ga! the plague
Rot them in hell!
Cramp! Ague! Pox! Gout! Stone — Hoo!
What shall I do to stop it?
It's sin — sin — sin. I hate them. Oog!
I want them to go groaning
Over imaginary ills
With white eyes twisted up to Me,
Where I sit and croak
And snarl. Ugh! Faugh!

I'm Yaugh Waugh!
I'm Yaugh Waugh!

Ga! Oa! Hoo! Hoo!
Scratch!
I must invent a plan
To ruin all this gladness.
Ha! Plup! I have it.
There's nothing here
That would accept my favours —
Uck! Bulch! —
So I'll abuse myself to chaos
And see what comes of it.
Ha — Ba! Ha — Ba!
Ab — ab — ab — ab — ab!
Utch — what is this?
Coagulated yolk of the addled egg
Of chaos! Hatch it out!
That's why I AM. Hoo — hoo — hoo — hoo — hoo!
Oh! — now the white of the old egg is curdled
Into a ragged fleece.
Ga! Ga! I've got a son:
What will it be?
O heaven — a lamb!
I'm Yaugh Waugh, Yaugh Waugh.
I'll call it Yaugh Shaugh Waugh.
Good! Can you talk,
Firstborn? — I'll never have another,
I'm Yaugh Waugh, Yaugh Waugh.
Bow to me, you lumpy lambkin!
Haw! Haw! Haw!
Now at last a wooden thing
That will do my business for me.
Uck! Uck! The morning's carrion
Bubbles in my paunch.

I am belching dreadfully.
What? Uck? Uck? How strange!
For the windy vomit of me
Shapes itself into a sorry
And bedraggled pigeon.
Birdie, have you got religion?
Yes, he bows most properly.
Come then, let us take our counsel
How to stop this sad behaviour,
This gross impropriety,
Irreligion — Uck! it's awful.
Squat, then! Pigeon, you're the youngest:
You speak first.

THE DOVE

Almighty father!
I have a magnificent
And sublime and noble scheme.
Listen! I will find a woman —

THE VULTURE

Oh! you dirty-minded rascal!

THE DOVE

Wait a moment — I will do it.
Find a virgin — if I can,
And on her beget this lambkin
In the image of a man.

THE VULTURE

That seems complicated, pigeon.

We've the lamb begotten here.

THE DOVE

Yes, I know; it seems absurd;
But in practice I am certain
It will work out splendidly.

THE VULTURE

Well, proceed!

THE DOVE

                                          Of course I will;
I'm accustomed to 'proceeding.'
Let the lamb grow up to manhood.
Then we'll have him whipped and tortured
And eventually killed.

THE VULTURE

That sounds lovely.

THE LAMB

                                      Do you think so?
I record my vote against it.

THE DOVE

Stupid! in a day or so
We will have you rise again.

THE LAMB

Really! I may be a dullard;
But I cannot see the point
Of this most elaborate nonsense.

THE DOVE

Well, you will. We'll make a rule
That anyone who disbelieves it
Shall be strictly prosecuted
— With the utmost rigour
Of the majesty of law.

THE LAMB

And if any fool believes it —

THE DOVE

He shall come to live with Us.
What a privilege!

THE VULTURE

                                                Provided

He observe propriety,
Never laugh, never dance,
Never do the dreadful thing!

THE DOVE

Precisely so!

THE VULTURE

It's settled then,
Charmingly unanimously
Carried by a show of wings.

THE LAMB

I protest.

THE VULTURE

You did not vote.

THE LAMB

If I had a pair of wings —

THE DOVE

You might fly; and so might pigs!

THE VULTURE

Pray, sir, do not mention pigs!
Gru — utch! Scheme approved, and entered in
The Minutes. I declare the board
Quite indefinitely adjourned.

THE LAMB

I oppose; I wish to enter
A minority report.

THE VULTURE

You are out of order, sir.

THE LAMB

I shall get my own back later
In the Theatres of London
Where a show of legs decides.

THE DOVE

By the way —

THE VULTURE

These sleeping women
Are no good to us, of course?

THE DOVE

No indeed! I want a creature
Very different to that,

THE VULTURE

Well, you'll have a job to find one.

THE DOVE

Would you lend me your red star?

THE VULTURE

With the greatest pleasure, pigeon!

THE DOVE

I'll be off, then.

THE LAMB

So will I.

THE VULTURE

I shall know where I can find you.

THE LAMB

Would you had a moment's patience!
I had a much better scheme
— One involving pigeon-pie!

THE VULTURE

Butch! be off with you. I'll hop
Up again to the tree-top.
Yaugh Waugh! That's me!
Always at the top of the tree!

(They depart separately, yet together. The old Philosopher wakes).

HERACLEITUS

Ah! but some evil things have brooded here
Over the sleepers. May it be indeed
The truth that some strange fate threatens the world?
That Art and Love and Beauty, to renew
Their glory, must be bathed in their own blood?

But who shall understand the Soul of Pan?
Involved in All and still apart from All!
For steeped therein as I am all my life,
I know but exquisite beatitude,
Knowing the whole, Then who shall know or care
What may befall the part? One must remain;
Many must change. Then all is well. The strife
Is but the ferment of the wine of life.
My task is simply to go forward still
Immune from grief, intolerant of ill,
Fronting the double foe — of pain and joy —
With equal eye — in the meantime —

                                                  Dear boy,

Wake! Let us revel it the while we may,
Love dawning ever with the dawning day.
Wake, brothers, sisters! It is time to stir.
The owl, the night-hawk, sad and sinister,

Have fled, The first flush animates the hills,
Reddens the rushes, flashes on the rills.
Come while the breeze blows and the air is cool
Down through the forest to the Fairies' pool.

(All rise and follow the sage, singing:)

THE COMPANY

    Praise Eros wittily!
      Praise Eros well!
    Tripping it prettily
      Down through the dell!
    Joyous and eager
      Our tresses adorning,

Away to beleaguer
  The city of morning!

Away to the leap to
  The soft-smiling pool
Whose kisses shall creep to
  Us virginal cool!
Race and bescatter
  The dew in the grass;
The nymph and her satyr!
  The lad and his lass!

O blest is the laughter
  Of Arcady's groves
That chases us after
  To delicate loves,
The frolics, the fancies,
  The fires, the desires,
The dives and the dances,
  The lutes and the lyres!

Follow, o follow,
  Sweet seed of the sun!
Through the wood, through the hollow,
  The race is begun
That shall fill the day up
  With the roses of pleasure,
The rod — and the cup —
  And the crown of our treasure!

Sweet are our voices;
  Our bodies are bare;
Their spirit rejoices
  Afloat in the air,

Coiling and curling
    In maze of the aeons
Its vision unfurling
    A pageant of paeans!

Blessed be Love in his
    Palace of praise
Whom we follow above in his
    Wonderful ways!
Whom we follow above
    To the stars and the snows,
Immaculate Love! —
    We adore thee, Eros!

Praise Eros wittily!
    Praise Eros well!
Tripping it prettily
    Down through the dell!
Joyous and eager
    Our tresses adorning,
Away to beleaguer
    The city of morning!

I

The Red Star

I

THE RED STAR

SCENE. — A grove of ilex in Arcadia. The terrace is of white marble. In the centre an image of the god Pan in Ivory and Gold. The pedestal is of lapis-lazuli, the space around of malachite. It is strewn with red roses. Before the image of the god stands a naked man, in whose hand is a sharp sword heavy and curved. Its blade is of blue steel, its hilt encrusted with rubies. The man is come to his full strength; he is very dark, with deep-set glittering eyes of green flecked with fire. His beard is short, square, curly, and black mingled with red. It is noon; the sun stands sole and supreme in the abyss of azure. The grove is completely hidden from the outer world by its ilex, and by the dark fastnesses of yew and cypress about it.

The man — Alexander, the great king — stands upright, facing the God, his arms raised as if to smite with the sword.

ALEXANDER

Naked I stand
    In the Garden of Pan.
Bare is the brand

29

That maketh a man.
The saying is said;
   The doing is done;
Bare is mine head
   To the fire of the sun.
But thou, o my Lord, are quiet and still;
And the feathers are clipt from the wings of the will.

Still are thy lips
   And void of motion,
Like red-sailed ships
   On a windless ocean?
Hast thou no lust
   To involve in a curse
The insane dust
   Of the universe?
Speak, o my Lord! I have journeyed afar
In the wake of the terrible crimson star.

A harp between mine hands,
   Murmurous and musical,
I come from far-off lands
   To seek Thee who are All.
Amid my warrior bands
   I rode in kingly wise:
Thy light upon mine eyes!

I came from very far
Led by that strange red star
At noon that fadeth now
Dim on the snow-crowned brow
   Of royal Caucasus,
A mystical portent
Of some obscure event
   Darkly miraculous

Written below the West
In Fate's dark palimpsest;
Obscure — the sun to eclipse!

I fed my flaming lips
Upon the limbs of slaves,
Great Nubian girls that bled
Upon the sands — so laves
The sun his fire in cloud
When the sea glows glassy red
At the buffet of the wind
On its cheek all wrinkle-lined.
Ah! thou Lord God! thus thrice
I made thy sacrifice.

Still thou art dumb,
Though I am duly come
Within thy secret grove
Naked and armless, save
For this seraphic glaive.
How then? What other price
May serve thy sacrifice?

Ah! by the evil glint
Of sun, portends an hint.
Shall I the childless king,
Chaste in thy praise, resign
That which was never mine,
The power of — spring?

Ay! by the fierce glad gleam
On thy dark lips, I see
Thy sober ecstasy
To watch the soft bright stream
Bubble and curl, like passion-flowers alight

On the seductive malachite,
To take with greedy joy
This — toy.
The jewels all-precious of a man
Waste death before thee — Pan!

   Steady I stare
Into Thine eyes' uxorious glare
Swimming with lust — as if I were
Some wandering Arab chief enthralled
By a sphinx with eyes of emerald,
As a bird fixed by an hissing asp,
As a maiden in a giant's grasp,
As a mariner caught in the viewless iron
And velvet vice of a singing siren!

I lift this blade to sheer
In one deliberate sweep
Of startling light
All that man holdeth dear.
From the sun's high steep to the great deep
Of unimaginable night
To dive — I dive.
Lord, now!
Pan! Pan!
Accept the supreme vow!
The man
Shall be no more a man —
Stay! who are these?

   (The stroke swings aside, as the pavement of malachite opens before him, at his feet, and two satyrs rise, with a little fair- haired child.)

From what barbaric seas
Ringing the icy North
Thus suddenly sprung forth
Come ye to mar mine — case?
For I was nigh at peace
With the great soul of things.

1ST SATYR

Hail, king of Kings!
It is our Master's will
That thou partake
Of — this!
So do the goat and snake
Dance on the pavement of sapphire
To the sound of the wind-haunted lyre.
And the light of a lewd understanding
Shines in them, and they lick their lips, and spill
Slaver of the stars! Hail, king! With Him fulfil
The sacrament of earth
Imperiously commanding
That leaps again to birth
At the divided flood
Of sun and rain. Arise!
The red gleam in thine eyes!
Up, up and slay!

2ND SATYR

Fair child,

Laugh thou; God honours thee
(Look! then, methinks, he smiled!)
To condescend to bless
That unripe loveliness.
The acid of thine immaturity

Shall be a sharpness in his mouth
Cloyed with too clinging sweet
Of the full-bosomed South.

1ST SATYR

Beside those rose-fair feet
Dimpled with fairy kisses
There's no bright-tinted bird
In all the blue abysses
Worth even a plumeless word.

THE CHILD

I do not like this place.
The god hath on harsh face.
Take me home now!

ALEXANDER (to the 1st satyr)

What next?

How shall a babe scarce- sexed
Avail when the dread offering
Of the world's mightiest king
Is not received?

1ST SATYR

Impale

You trembling fawn too frail
Upon that ivory ruby rod
That juts from the azure throne of God!
Then — as the scream chills the blue air,
Draw the curved steel along
The snow-pure throat! Hold the bright hair

Firm in one swarthy grip;
And ere the blood leap strong
Suck with insensate lip
That wine of Pan! Ah, drink!
Great king — as if the brink
Of Ganymede's own cup flowed over,
And thou, his languid lover,
Sank back into the arms of Zeus
With thine head hanging loose,
And the long curls adrip
With the dew oozing from his lip.

ALEXANDER

So! unto Thee! Come hither,
Child! You must pass before
Unto the land where all flowers wither
And the sea hath never a shore.

2ND SATYR

Ha! he hath dashed the babe to die,
And caught his first convulsive sigh
With a fierce kiss biting into his lips,
As a storm-fiend tears the reeling ships.
His fingers clutch the golden hair.
The head goes back, and the neck is bare.
Now for the sweep of the steel!

1ST SATYR

Pan! Pan!

THE CHILD

Oh mamma! mamma!

2ND SATYR

                                        Ha! what a man!
With a sweep he has severed the lamb-soft throat,
And the crimson blood in his cheeks afloat
Flames, an irradiate blaze to environ
Etna with mountains of molten iron.

ALEXANDER

Pan! o Pan! dissolve in bliss!
Take these severed lips to kiss!
Thou and I are partners of
This, the sacrament of love.
By the violate babe's blue eyes,
By his sucked-out arteries,
By the blood-bedabbled gold,
By the body void and cold,
Make me partner of thy power
Over this obscurest hour!

1ST SATYR

O the rich red blood that swims on
Over all the malachite!

2ND SATYR

Ah! the banquet gold and crimson
Like the sun afeast at night!

ALEXANDER

Out of the fume of the blood arise
Two lithe nymphs with amethyst eyes,

Sparkling with the wanton pleasure
That their small and laughing scarlet
Mouths betrayed, as overmeasure
Bubbled out the dancing harlot
Music of them, snaky slim,
Panther-smooth and light of limb
Wreathed with wealth of mystic berry,
As they leap, divinely drunken
On the very blood that gat them,
Insolent and lewd and merry
— With the satyr-eyes deep-sunken
Looking things prophetic at them!
Ah! my pan, if blood suffice,
Crush the world as in a vice!

1ST NYMPH

King of kings, the world shall bleed
In the vilest vice of vices.

2ND NYMPH

While the riddle thou hast ree'd
Mocks them with its "Blood suffices."

ALEXANDER

Know ye, bright ones, who I am?
I have slain a thing adored
At this altar to its Lord,
As a butcher kills a lamb.

1ST NYMPH

That shall be — thou rightly fearest —
Till the Balance weigh the Ram.

2ND NYMPH

Men shall even slay their dearest
For the sake of that slain lamb.

ALEXANDER

He was softer than a dove;
He was made for human love.
I have given him for food
To the lusty panic rood,
And the obscure brotherhood.

1ST NYMPH

So the doves of men begotten
Shall be plucked, and bruised, and rotten.

2ND NYMPH

So shall full-fed brothel-knaves
Kick them to indecent graves
In the name of the sweet Dove
That is God — for God is Love.

ALEXANDER

See ye naught but cruelty
In the infinite To-Be?
Look you, I have seen a star
Threatening pestilence or war
In the vault that hangs — a splash
Like a scar.

1ST NYMPH

From what a lash!

2ND NYMPH

O the monstrous travail-gape
In the belly of the sky!

1ST NYMPH

Shall the man beget the ape,
All the wine of time run dry?

2ND NYMPH

Ah! the grisly spoil of rape
Dark with vilest ecstasy!

1ST NYMPH

Listen, how shall life escape
From such death it breedeth by?

2ND NYMPH

Hangs there not a single grape
From that nightshade galaxy?

1ST NYMPH

Name the sharp accursed shape,
Stigma of its prodigy!

2ND NYMPH

Is it but a whirling storm?

ALEXANDER

Nay! the star is cruciform.

1ST NYMPH

Thus the holy cross is cloven
From Pan's purpose purple-woven.
Even for centuries nine and ten,
Life of women — death of men!
In that sinister sad star
Men shall bear the upright bar,
Hanged for honesty and truth,
Wisdom, courage, love, or youth.
Women bear the cross-bar, living
In the filth beyond believing.
Svelte or buxom, fair or dark,
Go to the maw of the greedy shark
Whose lascivious appetite
Is most swiftly set alight
By their beauty or their wealth,
By their passion or their weakness,
In sheer lust of hate, it may be;
In the open or by stealth,
By their slenderness or sleekness.
For harlot worn and blubbing baby
Nineteen centuries shall see
Life run horizontally.

2ND NYMPH

Soul shall follow body's station.
They shall cling to degradation,
Dance to the clank of the chains that eat
Deep ulcers in their fettered feet.
Lock love the dove in a close cage,
And loose the tiger marriage:
To the camel of joy be a needle's eye,
And a wolf's-throat to monogamy.
Youth's lusty god shall turn them sick,
While they dote on age's gilded stick.
Beauty shall shiver in the cold
While they warm their buttocks at the fire
Of lust and ugliness and gold,
The rank goats of the whorish mire.
So falls their flame to that decayed
Glow of wet rot in the wintry wood.
Ay! from this star disaster-rayed
A very wormwood draught is brewed:
The light of life shall shrink dismayed
At the dawn of prostitute and prude;
And the pagan glory fade
From the brows of womanhood.

1ST SATYR

But the boy shall thrust the maid
From the sunlight to the shade.
He shall make her passion good.

2ND SATYR

Nay! for all the world-decay
Rots from sapphirine to grey.

All the leprous lichen clings
Round the comeliness of things.
Brothers! Sisters! fauns and elves!
Dryads! Oreads! Undines!
Fairies, let us hide ourselves
In our innermost ravines
Inaccessible to man,
That our perfect peace in Pan
Hide from us the knowledge of
This eclipse of joy and love!

ALEXANDER

Is there nothing but distress
In the mystic vision lurking?

1ST NYMPH

Ah! but were thy loveliness
With the God supremely working!

ALEXANDER

Nymph, thy face is like a flower
Fairer than the driven foam!
Shining like an honeycomb
Is thy body — and thy soul
Shoots me to the gilded goal.
I shall master yet the hour.

SATYRS

King of Kings, we bow before Thee;
As our Master we adore Thee.
Grant us leave — the midmost wood

Calls us to its solitude.
We to bowers of flower and fern;
Thou to suffer — and to learn!

(They vanish, embracing the nymphs.)

ALEXANDER

I am alone —
— With Pan —
With the cold stone.
Nay! with the riotous god that ran
Through all, and conquered all,
And became all, and now is all.
— Oh matchless musical
Seven-throated god, I hear thy stridency
Like nereids playing on the wind-struck sea
That heaves herself with sensuous swaying!

I have seen a wild girl woven in gold
Stained with blue and scarlet — playing
Before me — she transported me
With the writhings of her painted hips
And her belly jerking up to my lips,
Into an azure abyss of sea,
With the sun glittering amorously.
But now, o Pan, the whole world falls
With its reeling rout of Bacchanals
Into the gulf, and thy wild note
Shrills up from the black Nothing's throat
Like an enchanted harp that playeth
Melodies, melodies magniloquent of death.
Yea! o thou golden wan strange-smiling one,
Thou art not only cold.
Thine ivory came from fierce bull-elephants

That trampled Persians in their battle-rage;
Thy gold was found by men most grave and sage
Among the sands of a strange river.
How my breast pants!
How my sides quiver!
Surely the breath of God is bubbling in
These veins, their blood that held its calm discourse
Lit with electric force
By Him for whom I have done sin,
Sin grievous against every part
To purge the whole through to the heart.
And lo! thine eyes that dazzle me
Like peacock's fans with many a million
Eyes of azure and vermilion
Each in its emerald pavilion
Like the death-god's majesty
Burning his ensanguine pain
In my blood, my heart, my brain.

Yea! with the scent of myrrh
And musk, and oliban, and strange perfumes
Begotten in pre-natal glooms
When all was — what? with infinite ambergris
The excellent kiss
Of Pan enshrouds me and invades.
See how the night-borne shades
Darken the grove!
There is no moon to-night
The foul red star blots out the stars.

So, Pan, thy love
That brooks not any light
Shall brand its shameful scars
Even on this flesh — this royal flesh shall serve
For the brute lust whose nerve

Shall eat up blindness in me, and discover
The mind of Pan, maker of all,
In all — his lover.

   Now still I stand entranced
And the faint fires that danced
Before the sunset like a vivid crown
Of blood upon thine head,
(O thou severe
And strong, my lover, my delight!)
Have all died down;
And in the darkness, clear
As the dawn's transient light;
Are thy lips, live at last;
Thine eyes, aflame at the red holocaust
Of me thou gloatest over.
See, I draw close,
(O vital, murder-loving lover!)
And all my being flows
In a flood to my lips, and I kiss kiss kiss
Madly, madly kiss,
Out of rhythm, out of rime,
Out of space, sense, time,
Thy mouth — and I am thine:
Sealed, sealed at last, enthroned upon
The very star thou ridest on.
O wine! o wine!
Wine of thy luminous body rushing, gushing,
Conquering, penetrating, crushing —
All the seeds of darkness in me
Splashed with fire and water,
So that spring arises in me
Like a warrior weary of slaughter
Striding to the striped lair
Of deftly-woven camel's hair,

Where the trembling captive-woman
Waits his pleasure-hour inhuman!
All the roots of love and power
Flushed at last into a flower.
All the films of sense dissolved;
All the spirit sight evolved,
So that after myriad aeons
Filled with trumpet-pealing paeans,
With the nuptial bliss of man
Prostituted unto Pan,
Rises on the vast inane
Your dread red star again!

O star, thy secret I possess:
I, watcher for man's happiness.
I go to ward thy craven curse
From the maiden Universe.

II
The White Wind

II

THE WHITE WIND

A bare volcanic desert. A foul lake stagnant in the distance. A crazy hovel on the edge of the squalid village. The clamour of Syrian dogs. A young girl stealing through the shadows of the moonless night, craftily.

THE GIRL

They have not stirred.
I am unseen, unheard.
Now for some honey of note
Plucked from the black lion's throat!
There is no moon: earth is too still.
A heat, yet bitter chill,
Is in the air, the windless air.
O for a breath of snow-wind on
The crest of Lebanon!
I would that boy that laughed
Upon me in the market would come by.
He twitched his robe awry,
And I beheld — ah! what a fatal graft
In that strange tree of youth! What gnarled and knobbed
Live tree throbbed, throbbed

With formidable threat — why did I fear?
What mystery encloses me?
My God! protect me! See
On the horizon what strange star awakes,
Like a gross lion that shakes
His tawny mane — and roars. Am I the prey?
See! like a tangle of black snakes
An evil smoke obscures the firmament
Belched from his throat! Now I repent
This mine adventure; I must creep, creep in —
I fear the night — oh day — day — come, sweet day!
Best was thy spur, the bloodied silver ache
That stings me like a snake,
The itch of blood, the shapeless thing that nestles
Between my baby breasts,
The lion lust that wrestles
With mine own soul — I understand so little —
Nay! not the tiniest tittle!
All that I know is this — the pangs consume
My maiden lily-bloom.
For all my cheeks are flooded with desire
And shame, and black foul fire
That bubbles in my soul, and shoots its terror
Out of these sloe-black eyes
Into the lake's unfathomable mirror,
That, laughing back upon me laughing, lies.
I will creep in — afar
From the frenzy of yon nameless star.

But who art thou
Descending in a cloud of cherubim?
A moon-white sickle crowns that flashing brow;
Thine head like the wise bird
Splendidly grim
That utters that unutterable word;

Thy body like the bright sun in his strength;
And all thy virgin length
Armed with the sword and balances,
Gold as the ultimate galaxies —

Thou art evanished.
Surely the Presence of the Lord wast thou
To utter forth some doom of dread —
But now?

(A young man in a white robe is found standing before her.)

THE YOUTH

Maiden, be comforted!
The Lord hath listened unto thy lament,
The ululation of that wolfish stress;
And I am sent
To heal thy loneliness.

MIRIAM

Ah! thou art not as he that saw me
To-day. Thou art comelier than he,
And softly mayest thou draw me
From this perplexity.
But hast thou — hast thou such a thing of fear
(Like an old giant's knotty spear)
As he? Thou dost not laugh and leer
As he did. No! I will not show my face

(She drops her veil.)

Stand back, stand back a space!

(She advances toward him.)

Nay, touch me not. I am a virgin vowed —

(She lays her hand upon his arm.)

I am of royal race
Most mortal proud —
    (She kneels, kissing his robe.)

Spare me, sweet sir!

(She pretends to stagger, and falls back upon the ground.
Her robe falls from her.)

THE YOUTH

I am a messenger.

(He disappears.)

MIRIAM

Shaitan! he slipped my grip.
Is there no flood to drip
Some icy liquor on this hell-scarred brow?
See! The red star glows fainter now.
All is a velvet heat of horror. Night
Holds me in torture.

                                        Hark! the lake

Stirs in its sleep; the ripples shake.
— Oh for the wind! Here naked will I lie
And let its coolness bite into my blood.
— Ho! What a whistle of wind
Whirling the spumy scud

Of the lake into a column of ecstasy!
Like a sharp spear it rushes up to me,
And in my face it flutters like a dove
Whispering strange words of love.
It sunders me! it cuts me — now, ah! touch!
These empty arms that grope, that strain, that clutch
Mere air, grow limp.....

                                    The wind is like a scythe
That cuts its swathe through my green field,
Even as I groan and writhe
In the agony that pierces to the marrow.
The wind! the wind! an arrow
That hath smitten me through the shield —
I float in mine own virgin tide
Let loose — ah! who are these that haunt me now,
Tumbling from the desert brow
Of the wild ensorcelled ridge,
Like a warrior's sacrilege;
Gnashing laughter sobbed or swelling
To a pestilence of yelling,
These gibbering apes that mop and mow
And leap upon me? Surely this is Fear
With face averted that constrains me to him —
And this blind worm is avarice. Let me woo him!
Sweet God! I'll serve thee. This is Piety
Twin-bodied with Hypocrisy that darts
His icy slime into my heart of hearts.
Here cringing Pity my wet womb inflates,
And puffed-out Charity with loose red cheeks
And greasy eyes. The Bigotry that sneaks
Home to my home; and once installed there, hates
The bleeding wound his mouth is fastened on;
And here is Chastity that slavering sates
His lust without the walls, grins, and is gone,
Preening himself that his lewd lips relent.

This must be Cunning that insinuates
His venom; this deformed and bent
Dog-like abortion, stinking excrement,
Is Slave-morality. Come all! I have
A lyre still tuneable to your great theme,
A pit as hospitable as the grave.
Come, dead and living! I am yours to-night.
Score after score! oh God — is this a dream?
Then let me never wake! Exhaustless might
Thrills me — as ever it shall — from the first thrust
Of that white wind whose steeltipped gust
Broke in my body to its lust.
What? Are ye done?

                             There is a distant chorus
Of robust voices; the earth heaves and pants
As if the seven and seventy elephants
Snow-white of Solomon made hither, marched
On the black earth sun-parched
Into the battle-front; grave and sonorous,
A clang of arms salutes these ears, that twitch
To catch the zenith pitch
Of aught that, human or divine,
Might pour some drowsy wine,
Poppy-heads bruised and seethed
In milk of asses ivy-wreathed
With honey and spice and wine moon-pale
Strained though a virgin's veil —
To ease this itch.

(Enter a Roman Centurion and his guard.)

THE CENTURION

Ha! Publius, saidst thou: "Jewish girls are chaste?"

PUBLIUS

Good — a barbarian Clodia Croup-in-air!

THE CENTURION

The brazenest whore in Syria, I dare swear!

PUBLIUS

Look at the blood! A very Hymen flare!

THE CENTURION

New meat to-night. She hath acquired the taste.
Come, friends, enjoy her. Have we time to waste?
I heard the cock crow.

(He embraces her rudely.)

PUBLIUS

Let it crow for her!

(One by one they defile her.)

MIRIAM

Scarce forty! Yet the dawn begins to stir:
The Wolf's tail blots my star. At last I strain
Some strength that strains my body back again.

THE CENTURION

Enough, lads! If she breed not, at my peril
I shall uphold it "Jewish girls are sterile."

MIRIAM

Stay, will you go? What, are you men — or tame?

PUBLIUS

Faugh, wench! is there no shame?

(He kicks her brutally. The guard moves off.)

MIRIAM

The dawn! oh, curses on the dawn that breaks
This night of joy. God! my whole being wakes
Into a world of rapture. I am I
At last — the little fool that wondered why!
I am abreast of God's whole tide of thought.
Like gold into fine linen, I am wrought
Into the royal vesture of the globe.
I am the Empress of the City of Sin,
Wrapped in its purple robe
Stained with mine own maid's blood.
Yea! for all glorious within
Am I, most like the daughter of a king,
Voluptuously languishing
Like a great queen afloat upon the flood
In gilded barge
On rugs of fur and silk
Broidered with curious device
Of basilisk and cockatrice

Upon the broad-woven scarlet marge.
— God! how this bosom boils with milk,
Its veined radiance swelling —
Ah! the light grows —
Back, from these splendid woes
And joys obscure
Into the squalid and impure
House, and the filth indwelling!

(She crawls within the hovel.)

III

The Blue Dwarf

III

THE BLUE DWARF

SCENE, a stable containing three stalls. In the first, an ox; in the second, the girl Miriam; in the third, the ass Zakariah. The first is chewing the cud peaceable; the second, stretched naked on the straw, holds her sides and groans; the third lifts up his voice ever and anon in a formidable bray. The stable is lighted by two torches held respectively by an old and withered hag, her two remaining teeth — long yellow fangs — exposed in a grin; and by a blue faced baboon, who revels in his corner in the filth.

THE HAG, addressing the baboon.

Ho! her time is not yet come;
We may dance together, dear.
Say, how beautiful art thou
With thy shining shame protruding!
Darling, apeling, why so glum?
Turn away that rosy sphere;
Show me the delicious brow
Ever brooding, ever brooding
Surely on my loveliness.

(They dance a jig together.)

Look at her obscene distress!
How it makes me laugh to see her
Writhing in her pains. — Come hither,
Mistress! join us, laughing freer
As thy lips and cheeks grow whiter,
And the old loves shrink and wither
At the kisses of the smiter!
Ho! Ho! Ho! a knock I hear...
By my maidhood, who comes here?

(The stable door is pushed in, and three holy kings appear,
surrounded by their retinue. They enter insolemn procession,
and seat themselves at the central stall.)

GOVINDA

Say, my brother, is the vision
That thou sawest in the grove
Answered?

CHAU

Doth the exact division
Of the azimuth rightly prove
That the star points hither truly?

ALEXANDER

Brothers, all is proven duly.
Memory joins with astrolabe:
This the maiden — hers the babe.

MIRIAM

Who are ye? I would be alone.

Now the loose and heaving zone
Frets me. Go, my mates, carouse
With the cuckold of the house
With his adze and awl and chisel!
Zakariah with gilded pizzle
And this bull grown sleek and smooth
To an ox suffice, in sooth,
Love's exalted task — and thus
Kings are grown superfluous.
Ai! but now the monster splits me
Struggling in his bloody cage.
Is it in his sport or rage?
Answer that, thou doting sage!
For his cacodaemon shape
Twisting round no longer fits me.
This is like some hellish rape
Of one's soul the grisly ape!
Get ye forth to Aggereth
Riding in her golden car
Yoked to ox and ass that prance
In their evil Hinnom-dance!
I am writhing with my death
Born of the infernal Star.

ALEXANDER

Nay, our lady, we are come
    To thy worship — high and holy;
From our heaven-wide halidom
    To the manger dark and lowly
We have brought taraxacum,
    Mandrake, amrit, myrrh and moly;
        Many a royal gift of gree
        From the land of Danae,

From the coral-breeding sea,
From the steppes of Tartary!

GOVINDA

I have brought a treasure-chest
Full of gold, red gold galore,
All a pirate's hoarded store
From the islands of the West
Gathered far with blood and tears
For three score and seven years.
All this wealth of virgin gold
This thy babe shall helt and hold.
He shall buy the souls of priests;
Forge men chains, and make them beasts;
Give the carrion soldier meat,
And corrupt the judgment-seat.
With it he shall seethe the snake
Of his faith in fire-hot blood;
Hurt the humble, strew the stake
With the faggots; gild the rood
That for many a year shall brand
With its blight full many a land.

CHAU

I have brought him frankincense.
He shall dull therewith the sense
Of his slaves, that they may be
Docile in their slavery.
He shall fill their aching minds
With the smoke that madness finds
The sole cloak of anarchy.
   Misty vapours demon-wrought
   Fill the cold clear dome of thought.

ALEXANDER

Mother, I have brought him myrrh.
Sorrow black and sinister
Shall his name bring to the race.
Wheresoever on the earth
Shall be heard his hissing name
Shall be madness and disgrace,
Falsehood, barrenness, and shame
For the folk of praise and worth.
    All the pure, the fair, the young
Shall taste curses on his tongue;
But the old, the chill, the base,
Shall find beauty in his face.
    Also, of Astarte's fruit
We have brought him orchis root.
Cinquefoil, and musk, and fins
Of the turtle and the shark
Scraped with damiana-bark,
Every grain a score of sins!
    In this flask of crystal lurks
Bruised virility of Turks,
Boiled with wine and ambergris —
Every drop an hour of bliss!
    This cornelian box contains
Datura-seeds and sparrow-brains,
Mixed and smoothed with asses' fat.
    Here the marrow of a bat
Concecrated by a wizard
And the seed-cells of a lizard
Banned by a Thessalian witch,
Lie like twins — royally rich
In this casket wrought with gems
Fit for Mogul diadems.

MIRIAM

O dogs, kings, gods, begone!
Bone splits from bone.
I am ripped up like a sweating sow
On the horn of a buffalo!
What care I for your gifts, unless
They might relieve this wretchedness?
God! I am split asunder
Like a cloud by a clap of thunder!

GOVINDA

The sweat is on thy forehead like bright stars
Amid the milk of the galaxy.

CHAU

Thy body gapes like a valley of deodars
Between two snowy hills in Tartary.

ALEXANDER

Ho! Ho! a million rats
Herald the brat's
First yelp.

(A vast company of rats issue from her, and rush squeaking
into the darkness.)

MIRIAM

God be mine help!
Adrammelek exacts a death
For every dance with Astoreth.

GOVINDA

Cling to the ass-god, queen!
Now while his loud obscene
Bray deafens us — now cling
To the lewd stark dripping thing
Thou has caressed and gilt
From the point to the gross hilt
With the babe-gold of thy bright skin,
Wolfing it in
As the dragon swallows up the moon!

CHAU

See, she will swoon.
This is magnificent.
I would not lose the event —
Ho! boy, bring wine! Black wine in jars of jade
Cooled all these months in hoarded snow!
Black wine with purple starlight in its bosom,
Oily and sweet as the soul of a brown maid
Brought from the forenoon's archipelago,
Her brows bound bright with many a scarlet blossom —
Like the blood of the slain that flowered free
When we met the black men knee to knee!

ALEXANDER

Brothers, how found you me?

GOVINDA

I have a gipsy girl
Skilled in the mystic art.
She knows the trick to curl
Dried leaves in fire, and augur thence.
I bought her in the mart
From an old Greek — a vile old man!
He told me she was a Bohemian;
And by a fabulous conjuring with cards
Indeed she can divine.

CHAU

                                    So can our bards.
These girls are shifty.

GOVINDA

                                    Maybe so; but list!
(I pray you) She can take an amethyst
And see a thousand visions.

CHAU

                                            So can I
When the wine fills me. Pray you!

   (His slave presents wine to Govinda, who drinks.)

GOVINDA

                                    Health, my lord!
This wine is marvellous dry!

Scented like clover reaching up the broad
Edge of some glacier in my northern marches.

CHAU

Look, how she writhes — speechless distemperature
Her shriek within her gorge that parches!

GOVINDA

Boy, bid that cup-slave from Ferozapur
Make me an ode of this — nay, while I think!
An elegy.

CHAU

Please your majesty to drink?

GOVINDA

Thanks, brother. Well, my gipsy girl divined
The purport of the star we saw enshrined
In the eclipse — to say so — of the sky.
I feared her perfidy;
The journey might prove tedious — (nay, my lords!
Star or no star, I am honoured, glad, to find
Such royal mates!). But her, I had her stripped
And most magnificently whipped
By two tall slaves (a Tartar and a Goth)
Till all the flesh was ripped
From her olive back — she looked like a dead camel
When a man frightens off the kites;
And her rich blood came all afroth
To her lips' vermeil enamel
— The lips that I had kissed!

And still she would persist.
   You see, she had her rights;
For here am I come — a feast I had not missed
Willingly, for a thousand beads of jade,
Or a broad-hipped Nubian maid,
Or a diamond flask of rose-perfume,
Or a Shiraz boy in his first best bloom!
Oh, I rewarded her well altogether,
For she slept at my feet through the cold mountain weather.

CHAU

I who am come from the remote abode
Beyond the highest snows,
Beyond the swiftest river,
Was moved thereto by a strange goad —
Stranger, my lords, than all your wisdom knows!
For in the city of gold and jade
Beyond where my vassal Tartars shiver
I have a dagger gold-inlaid
Sharp as an arrow from the heavenly quiver;
Its hilt of clustered fires, a crusted jewel
Fashioned in the likeness of a demon-king
Most exquisitely cruel: —
Daily I try my luck
By the Oracle of the Bleeding Duck.

GOVINDA

Look! what a horrid horde of toads
Hops from the Syrian wench!

   (Toads, issuing from the maid, hop off croaking into the
darkness.)

MIRIAM

Ah! ribald croak!
Intolerabe stench!
Spasm on spasm of agony still goads
My soul to get to God.

GOVINDA

The third should be the final period.
What portent may we look for?

ALEXANDER

By this dial

We must wait yet a little, majesties!

CHAU

I tell you of the Oracle. I took
(So that it might be an exhaustive trial)
A snow-white bird with purple tail-feathers
Wherein pale flames of gold mingled and shook.
Here, too, my wisest ministers
Gathered to solve the riddle of the Star.
But so the balky brute
Crushed in this gnarled fist
Maintained the unequal war
That at the dagger-sweep
Strongly she leapt — I missed!
And all my joy and all her crimson flux
Sprang in a mingled river to the West.

GOVINDA

See how she tears her breast!

CHAU

She is like a wounded horse
Gored by some old rogue-elephant.
For now the mouth springs open, and a yell
Like the shriek of the throat of hell
Bursts, and is choked by a vomit of black worms.

ALEXANDER

All this most critically confirms
Our calculations. Boy! the long pale glass
Fashioned of ambergris and chrysopras.
Fill it with the old, the ripe Satyrion,
And bear it to their Majesties. Anon
We shall see? —

GOVINDA

Sure, a son

CHAU

I wager thirty loads of merchandise
Most precious — sandalwood and gold and spice
And jewels, and divine medicaments,
And goat-hair broideries, and silken tents —
And thirty diamonds of the purest water,
It is a daughter!

ALEXANDER

I take it — and yours too, my lord. Maybe
You both are wrong.

GOVINDA

True, this much mystery
Veils the whole matter — it were hard to say.

CHAU

Shang Ti! how fierce a bray
The amorous ass gives.

MIRIAM

Heave, o heave, my sides!
Stretch! Split! This pang decides
For life or death. Now! — — Stretch! —
Plague on the wretch!
Friends, ease me — with a scimitar!

ALEXANDER

We learnt not that from the dark Star.

MIRIAM

Why then, be cursed!
My belly is about to burst.

(The hag and the baboon come forward.)

THE HAG

Ho! we will lift the prudish latch.
Dear apeling, hold the torches while I catch
This monster. So. Dispatch!

MIRIAM

God! let it be a boy.
I would enjoy
His love.
Who hath come forth with such keen pain
Owes keener pleasure, going back again.
A curse upon that Dove.
Whose windy letch hath blown me out
Like a rich man with flatulence and gout!

THE HAG

Ho! stanch thy throttle!
Come forth!

   (She delivers her.)

   O jest insane!
For all this pious pain
Naught but an old brass bottle!

GOVINDA

Maybe it holds the two and seventy Jinn
That Solomon screwed in.

ALEXANDER

More like, the wine that Dionysus spilled
From Cyprus grapes distilled.

CHAU

We lose our wagers? It may be
Best to unscrew it, and to see.

MIRIAM

Have ye no pity, kings, at this disease?
O then I am a mere muck-midden of shame.
But yet my body feeds on flame
As if some masterpiece
Were wrought — I know not how — pray cease!
Leave me with these!

GHAU

Midden or maiden, we must see the birth
Of thy black womb.
Why do these moans disturb our mirth?
I will have thee lashed to shreds
By this vile groom
Unless thou quit thy prating.

THE HAG

Here's pay for months of waiting.

(She detaches the placenta.)

A black old rotten wine-skin, mangy goat
Patched with bat, stork, and stoat!

ALEXANDER

Here come the bottle back, washed bright.
Yes, this is certainly the seal
Of Solomon.

GOVINDA

I feel
That we are on the brink of some strange sight.

CHAU

The whole event has seemed improbable.
Scribes, you record this well!
Or I will have you sliced with the keen steel
My cook keeps razor-sharp for salted swine.
Nine thousand cuts, nine hundred cuts,
And ninety cuts and nine
Cut exquisitely fine,
And the last slash in your guts
If by an hair's breadth your recital
Obscure the true, omit the vital!

ALEXANDER

Out springs the screw.
Ho! the mannikin slim and sprightly
Dressed in a neat surtout of blue
With the head of a goat and the nose of a Jew
And the...

GOVINDA

Would your Pasiphae challenge him lightly?

CHAU

Truly, a marvel. Come, little man!
We kiss your hands, and sail back home
Over the desert and over the foam.

ALEXANDER

And I go back to the grove of Pan.

GOVINDA

What is thy name?
I will proclaim
Thy marvellous fame
From the Gulf of Kutch to the shores of Orissa.

MIRIAM

I pray your Majesty, call him Issa.

THE BABE

Nay! I am come to the hour appointed.
Anoint me, sirs, and call me 'Anointed!'

GOVINDA

Rather be Baa-Baa called, for thy jerkin
Is a fleece like his friends wrap an holy Turk in,
When he twirls on his toes
Regarding his nose
Or his paunch that would hold a firkin!

THE HAG

The little beast is double-jointed.
Dance a spring, thou springal strutting
Like a stag in the glades at the season of rutting!

ALEXANDER

Dance, o thou imp
   Of the bottle of brass
With the hag and the pimp
   And the ox and the ass!

GOVINDA

Dance, o thou mannikin
   Dwarf and malign
To the clink of Earth's pannikin
   Drained of its wine!

CHAU

Dance, to the scream
   Of strangled humanity,
The delirious dream
   Of the Vampires of Vanity!

(The kings rise, bow, and depart.)

THE KINGS

Away, away like the wanton wind!
One to the groves of ilex tall;
One to the plains of infinite Ind;
One beyond the Mongol wall.
As we met, so we part.
Three great kings and one true heart!

IV

The Black Bean

IV

THE BLACK BEAN

SCENE - A small Syrian mud nut. On a truckle bed strewn with dirty straw lie a naked man and woman.

MAGDA

Give me more money, Baa-Baa, for a kiss;
One of my kisses.

ISSA

Youdesh has the bag.
(A pause.)

Also I weary of thy sordidness.
Love is at bottom a most noisome hag.
Mother and brothers! all the pageant passes
Like a loud caravan of braying asses;
And now I — love thee! in this hole of hell.
A rotting camel by a dried-up well!

Pah! but the brothel-reek contaminates.
There is no air — thy bed is poisonous,

Thy breath — thy leper-life lascivious —
Fill me with loathing. Murder-waking hates
Surge in upon me as I see thee there
Wanton and white in that red touzle of hair
As if a sow were wreathed with poppy-flowers.
Pah! I am sick of these delirious hours.
John's lips are cool like olive-oil — and thine,
Even at the best, like some black stormy wine.

MAGDA

Oh beast thou art! Didst thou not surely quicken me
With child?

ISSA

Thy lewdness and thy lowness sicken me.
Nay, let the heavy-fringed purple lashes
Lie still — my lust is burnt to bitter ashes!
The wrinkled eyepits black with grime and kohl
Are like black bogs to suck away my soul.
The coarse vermilion on thy cheeks is fire
Of hell to blast the charred stump of desire.
The blue tattoo-marks stain thy mouth like bruises;
The fat creeps on thy body as it chooses,
Fighting the leanness of thy lechery
That hags thee — Faugh!

MAGDA

Art thou not lewd with me?

ISSA

Ay! and the rot of Egypt pays me for't.

MAGDA

To match thy rotten soul, thou pimping ort!
Marrowless bone! Dry fig!

ISSA

Enough, black bitch!
The Seventy shall stone thee for a witch.

MAGDA

More than enough. I'll call thy darling itch,
Thy —
   (He fists her in the abdomen.)

ISSA

   Take the name back to thy bloated belly!
Speak, and I kick thy carcass to a jelly!

MAGDA

Thou empty bottle of brass of Bethlehem!
John, come and loose this surly saviour's phlegm!

   (John descends a rickety ladder from a loft. Magda spits,
and goes out.)

JOHN

Hail, master, let me soothe thy time of teen!

ISSA

Wine rots the liver; fever swells the spleen;
Meat clogs the belly; dusts inflames the eye:
Stone irks the bladder; gout — plague — leprosy!
Man born of woman is most full of trouble;
God a gorged fool that belches him, a bubble! —
But of all plagues wherewith a man is cursed,
Take my word for it, woman is the worst!

JOHN

Maybe, dear Lord, of all the words men say
Of thine, that one shall never pass away.
But what hath the wench done?

ISSA

                                          Undone me quite,
Nagged me with sordid greediness all night,
Greed for my gold, my person — all I have.
Saith not the prophet: "Cruel as the grave?"
That grinning mask, that musk-rat, hath enriched
Her rags by every inch of me that itched;
And for one itch hath planted me another,
The "friend that sticketh closer than a brother."
Ten groans of mine for every grin of hers!
What saith the prophet? — "Whited sepulchres!"

JOHN

Nay, Lord, the phrase unique is all thine own.

ISSA

Then write it down, an nothing less atone.
And add — of all the itches that breed bile
No itch beats the papyrus and the style.

JOHN

Hast thou no love for me, Lord?

ISSA

   Yes, lad, yes.
— Tinged through with many-coloured bitterness!
For as I lay this night of hateful heat,
The blow-flies buzzing, the eternal bleat
Of strayed sheep, the intense malefic hum
Of the accurst mosquito, the far drum
Of the winged beetle, the reiterate stings
Of fouler vermin, the hot breath that brings
The sunset's garlic to the midnight's rose,
The red whore's writhings, clutches swift to close
On this worn limb, exact the woman-debt
To the last mite, the cold grey glutinous sweat
— These things, I say, assailed me, bade me pause
Praising the goodness of the great First Cause.

JOHN

Yet all we know His vast benevolence.

ISSA

Thou hast religion, but no common sense.
The cud of wisdom is not duly chewed
When whoredom's whittled with a platitude.

JOHN

The upshot?

ISSA

I am sick of everything.

JOHN

Of me, Lord?

ISSA

Thou the least, sweet queen and king.
But — finally — in sooth, lad — even of thee.

JOHN

Lord, have I failed in love?

ISSA

                                 Failure must be.
Not by thy fault, but fixed in every feature
Of Mistress Smirking Whore, our Mother Nature,
Whose filthy dugs our poisoned kisses suck.
Pah! the whole world is just a mass of muck.

JOHN

Wait, master! that's a Phrase.

ISSA

                                        Take note of it:
Matter is muck!

JOHN

True wisdom and true wit!
The upshot, Lord?

ISSA

Than living, I would rather
Play the fool's game of my unnatural Father.

JOHN

Thy father, Lord? Thy pardon, but we heard —
ISSA

No odds — all genealogy's absurd.

JOHN

Suppose, Lord, I should simply call Thee "Word?"

ISSA

Happy the thought! But, in thy secret ear,
There was a scheme — thou mark'st me?

JOHN

                                        Crystal clear.

ISSA

I came from heaven.

JOHN

We guessed it.

ISSA

Guess again!

What follows?

JOHN

— Er —

ISSA

To humbug me is vain.

Guess!

JOHN

Well, to come from heaven — Thou com'st to reign?

ISSA

I die — thou mark'st me?

JOHN

Truly: plain as plain!

ISSA

And then, to counterbalance the effect —
What next?

JOHN

I cannot say.

ISSA

I resurrect.

JOHN

What good would that do?

ISSA

As I understand,
It would spoil life for everyone.

JOHN

How grand!
How simple!

ISSA

Look, boy, I am tired of things.
Joy, that had legs before, hath now got wings.
I am exceeding weary.

JOHN

Even of me?

ISSA

Yes — no — yes — what thou wilt. All's one.

JOHN

I see.

Then thou wilt slay thyself?

ISSA

'Twere too much trouble,
Having cut the corn, to clear away the stubble.
Hire thou a knave to slay me.

JOHN

Lord, I dare not.

ISSA

Denounce me to the Seventy — I care not.
Indeed, since Death is Death, small odds the plan of it!
I'll rather choose to get what fun I can of it.

JOHN

I have it, Lord! We'll make thy death suggest
Adonis, Attis, Mithras, and the rest;
And if there lack some detail —

ISSA

Thou art wise

Enough to write in all the prophecies
Fulfilled. That's settled, then.

JOHN

I'd love to see
The goggling eyes of duped posterity,
Its mouth agape (while priests scoop out its poke)
At the wild sequel of our harmless joke.

ISSA

Only one further fret balls up my brain:
— The nuisance, if I have to rise again.

JOHN

Fear not! The style suffices.

ISSA

Then be off,
And tell the Seventy my bitter scoff
At their phylacteries, my clever stroke
At God, my break-and-build-the-temple joke:
And make the fell indictment yet completer
With my bewildering pun on 'rock' and 'Peter!'

JOHN

It shall be done.

ISSA

Nay, thou wouldst feel remorse.
Let the whole matter simply take its course!
Our Youdesh is a theif; so, sure to rat.
He'll raise their camel to conceal his gnat.

JOHN

How choice a metaphor! How terse! How dry!
Apt as thy 'camel and the needle's eye.'

ISSA

Agreed, then! Now if Brothers Louse and Bug
Will let me be, I'll settle slack and snug
Till noon.

JOHN

I too, Lord, I would sleep with Thee.

ISSA

Lie down, then! On thine oath, no knavery!

JOHN

Sleep well, dear master! Kiss me!

ISSA

Pah, young thickhead!

(The door opens.)

No peace, saith someone somewhere, for the wicked!

(Enter Magda.)

What is it now?

MAGDA

If Rabbi Pip is gone,
It's Back to Bed!

(Issa wearily rises.)

ISSA

Then — Back to Bed with John!

JOHN

What, wilt Thou go?

ISSA

                                        Yea, by the holy hem
Of Aaron's robe — off to Jerusalem!

(He goes out, followed by the protesting pair.)

V

The Grey Night

V

THE GREY NIGHT

SCENE. — The thick darkness of the Emptiness of Things. Yet in the midst appears a certain glory veiling the figure of a tall stern man, the King Alexander. In his hand is a black rod clothed with twin glittering snakes, the royal Uraeus serpents of ancient Khem; at its point gleams faint and blue a star of six rays, whose light now illuminates the pale and tortured features of a man, with outstretched arms, who is hanging (apparently) in space. It is Issa, but the weariness is gone; and noble-strong is the scarred brow of his agony.

ALEXANDER

In the puissance of my will,
Issa, I uphold thee still.

ISSA

Thou art?

ALEXANDER

Keeper of the Way.

ISSA

I am?

ALEXANDER

Man, at mine essay.
By the Balance reaching forth
To the South and to the North
Have I consecrated thee
Co-victim with humanity.

O misbegotten, miscreate
Dwarf as thou wast, the child of hate;
Thou who hast felt the sordidness
Of thine own effect on thine own distress;
Art come thereby to the stature of man
By my power, who am Pan.
And by this death shalt laugh to know
Thy father's final overthrow.

My soul the heights and depths hath spanned.
I hold the star-stream in mine hand.
I am the master of life and death
And of every spirit that quickeneth.
Yea! in the light of knowledge, Pan
Hath grasped at the blackness of the ban:
And thus do I crush it. As the storm
Whirls shrieking round thy ghastly form
Thy spirit's torture shall abate
The bodily pangs of thy fearsome fate.
Weak fool! The fate of Arcady
And the whole world — that hung on thee!
Hadst thou but made thee Emperor,
And led thy legions into war!

Thou broken reed — a birth unclean,
A life sucked up in sordid spleen
A death absurd, most foully wrought
To the shape of thy father's leper-thought.
This be thy doom, that thou shalt see
The curses that are born of thee!
Thou black bat that hast barred the sun
From the sight of man, thou minion
Of death and disease, of toil and want,
Of slavery, knavery, greed and cant,
Of bigotry, murder, hypocrisy
— Speak thou the things that are seen of thee!

ISSA

Canst thou not save me, Pan,
And balk the bestial plan?

ALEXANDER

I too have died to Pan, and he
Hath begotten upon me
A secret wonder that must wait
For the hour of the falling of thy fate,
Nineteen centuries shalt thou
Plague earth with that agonizing brow,
And then that age of sordid strife
Give place to the aeon of love and life.

A lion shall rise and swallow thee,
Bringing back life into Arcady.
So strong shall he roar that the worlds shall quake
And the waters under the heaven break,
That the earth, of the father's hate accurst,
Shall be greener and gladder than at first,

ISSA

I shall endure then, if the Ultimate
Be reached through the black fate.

ALEXANDER

Let that sustain thee — yet this hour
I put forth all my torture-power
To grind thee in mills of martyrdom,
That at last thy spirit may fully come
To understand and to repent —
Else might thy new-born strength relent
And all thy father's hate corrode
Thy will, as the breath of a bloat toad
Might rot the lungs of a young child.
Then were indeed the earth defiled
And the sole seedling that must lurk
In the desert world - waste by thy Work -
Itself its loveliness transplant
To a flawless field whose grace should grant
Life to that bright inhabitant.

ISSA

These eyes are blind with blood and tears;
They strain across the doubtful years;
They search the stars: the earth they scan;
All, all spells Misery to Man.

Of whom I am. First, fables gross and foul
Hooted and hissed by human snake and owl
About me, twisted into doleful engines
Of greed, hate, envy, jealousy and vengeance.

Next, scythes laid to the root of every flower
That asks but sunshine for its brief glad hour.
Next, axes at the root of every tree
That strains its top to immortality.
Yea, o thou terrible magician,
I see the black wings of suspicion
Fanning each ear with tales of spite,
Blasting each bud with bitter blight.
I see the poisonous upas-tree,
Its shade the ghastly trinity
— Religion, law, morality —
Sicken with its stifling breath
Human loveliness to death.
I myself the tool of priests,
Tyrants, merchants, hags, and beasts,
Lawyers, doctors, artizans,
Whores and theologians!
All my life misunderstood
Built in slime, and nursed with blood!
This my death divinely hallows
Boot and rack, stake and gallows.
Strong men crushed beneath my domes,
Children tortured in my homes,
Women tricked and raped and herded
In the stinking stye bemerded
With the putrid excrement
Of the marriage sacrament.
Every scourge and sore and shame
Blest in mine accursed name!
Love and beauty under ban!
Wit and wisdom barred to man!
Nature smirched by hideous lies!
Meanness lauded to the skies!
Pain and ruin and disease
Praised, as if they made mine ease.

Dead be dance and dream and revel!
Thought and courage, things of evil!
Corn and milk, wine and oil,
The guerdon of degrading toil!
Life's bright draught of honied leisure
Soured to sick and tasteless pleasure.
All the gracious grape degraded,
To a fatuous foulness faded;
Ecstasy divinely deep
Bartered for a brutal sleep
In whose grunting crapulence
They may forget the glory whence
They came, and hide in a stinking slum
The beastliness they have become.
    Wealth complaining in its stye!
Stark starvation standing by!
Poet, painter, sculptor, sage
Prostituted to their age;
Or starved or tortured, should they hold
To the clear sunlight and the age of gold,
— Scarce a tithe of all I see,
Yet — thou dost not pity me?

ALEXANDER

Thou art near death: thy corpse light dawns on us.
See! the tenebrous glare and venomous
And all it shews. Enough! I leave thee, man,
To hide me in the secret place of Pan
Beneath the fallen groves Arcadian.

(He fades away, as if the new light, making the filth visible,
made him invisible.)

ISSA

I am nailed here too fast: —
I strain in agony aghast;
For I have blotted out the sun
From the sight of everyone.
With me on either hand lie slain
— Ah! never more to rise again! —
Virtue and beauty. Dark and dank,
The low hill's baked and barren bank!
There at my feet the glib scribe scrawls
His flatulent gnostic caterwauls
For gaping agapic festivals.
By him the red-haired harlot sprawls,
And the blotchy beast that suckled me
Squats like a toad, and shamelessly
Ogles the crowd of bystanders
With those wicked glittering eyes of hers.
Perched high above me the foul bird
My father belches his lewd word,
Triumphant in his scheme's success
That binds the globe in bitterness.
Blithe, the hag and the baboon
Frisk it to the tuneless tune
Of a sow that drums upon
A half-rotted skeleton.
Round me stretch the busy lines
Of architects at their designs —
Brothels, jails and hospitals,
Legislatures, arsenals,
Churches — towers and spires and domes,
Houses — nay! but the white tribe's homes
Whose chalky skins shall match their shores,
While their itching prudes and satiate whores
Bear — strange fate! — in that puritan den

The goodliest graft of the race of men
'Mid the ruck of hypocrite and slave
That grovel and groan from the womb to the grave.
Sadly keeping watch and ward
Are the century and his guard.

AGRIPPA

These portents much oppress me.

PUBLIUS

                                                    Bodes
Also my soul.

AGRIPPA

   Such anger goads
My spirit at this strange black time.
— This duty hath the eyes of crime!

PUBLIUS

Duty insists.

AGRIPPA

   But fear persuades.
— This deathly light, these foul grey shades!

PUBLIUS

Portending little enough of good
To Rome, that beats with our heart's blood.
See how dejected on their spears
The guard lean!

AGRIPPA

Rather a thousand years
Of strife than this black peace. Accurst
I know this night shall be.

ISSA

I thirst.

AGRIPPA

Give him to drink!

PUBLIUS

How strange a fate!
Those noble eyes irradiate
This leprous lustre.

AGRIPPA

See, the foul
Black thing that sits with sneer and scowl!
Over his head.

PUBLIUS

What now? Beshrew
Me, but its face is like a Jew!

YAUGH WAUGH

Butch! The game is fairly started.
I will back to night and chaos. — Ha! Hoo!

Formlessly presiding
Over the ruined earth.
Ga! Ga!
Ab — ab — ab — ab — ab —
  (He flies off.)

ISSA

Behold! he hath forsaken me.
The doom is fixed, but my spirit is free
From his loathsome company.

AGRIPPA

What was that cry?

1ST SOLDIER

I hardly heard it.

2ND SOLDIER

I heard, sir, but I could not word it.

MAGDA

I understood, my lord.

AGRIPPA

Well, slattern?

MAGDA

He called for a prophet.

PUBLIUS

A Priest of Saturn

That is, I fancy. These barbarians
Are really like our Unitarians.

AGRIPPA

So I have heard. Last year I flirted
With Isis — but was unconverted.
If this man's prophet loose my nails
I'll gibe no more at prophet's whales.

PUBLIUS

I loathe and despise all kinds of fiction
Whether or no it ease life's friction.

AGRIPPA

Anoint the next fair lambkin's fleece
With rock-sand in the stead of grease!

PUBLIUS

He speaks again.

ISSA

Forgive me, brothers!
I knew not what I did.

PUBLIUS

His mother's
Here; wants the body.

AGRIPPA

She must have
An order from the prefect.

MIRIAM, to a bystander.

Knave,
Wilt earn a penny? Beg this grace,
For the death-dews stand on the bloodless face.

1ST BYSTANDER

What is the name of the criminal?

A GREEK DISCIPLE FROM ALEXANDRIA

Say,
Logos, or Homoniousios!

JOHN

Nay,
Fool! Homoousios - lippis et nota!

THE GREEK

Homoiousios, with the iota!

JOHN

Nay, thou Greek heretic devil, have done!
Before He is dead is a schism begun?
Say Homoousios!

THE GREEK

Never, dog Jew!
Homoiousios!

JOHN

Master, decide!

ISSA

O may I cease! if my spirit to you
I must commend.

JOHN

Are you now satisfied?
Clear as —

THE GREEK

You lie, pathic!

JOHN

                                  Pandar!

THE GREEK

                                  Demented!

JOHN

Here is the argument Ehud invented!

(He thrusts a dagger into the belly of the Greek disciple
from Alexandria. The dirt comes out. To the Bystander,)

Say Homoousios!

PUBLIUS

Surely they will
While his logic is backed with such surgical skill.

TWO BYSTANDERS

We fly to do as you desire us.

JOHN

And bring me up a clean papyrus!
These chapters will make of no account
The ridiculous sermon on the mount.
Where was I? With twelve aeon-chains
Somewhere revolving in these brains;
Synoches, teletarchs, iynges,
All turning as smoothly as if on hinges:
Identity of Father and Son
And a Comforter, comforting everyone
Who reads the beautiful message of John!

AGRIPPA

Know, I can hardly hold myself in.
The whole scene tests our discipline
Somewhat too harshly. Were it not best
For a soldier to run him through the breast?
We should be free for a bath and a meal.

PUBLIUS

Sir!

AGRIPPA

I know well; but I somehow feel
My backbone slacked to the writhe of a worm.

PUBLIUS

The perfect would know how to keep you firm
At the cost of a handful of nails — up there!

AGRIPPA

Tis the influence of this filthy glare.
Stronger it grows.

PUBLIUS

How very surprising,
For the sun shews devil a sign of rising!

AGRIPPA

The guard should have come an hour ago
To relieve us.

1ST SOLDIER

By Zeus! 'twas a foul throw!

2ND SOLDIER

Throw again!

3RD SOLDIER

It's Venus! the coat is mine.
Silky-soft and rainbow-fine!
Would the world were never duller
Than this cool cascade of colour!

AGRIPPA

Something serious is occurring.
All the town is lighted, stirring.
We had best bring reinforcement.

PUBLIUS

Death was duty's one divorcement.

AGRIPPA

Pooh! the stern old Roman! Fudge!
Even Horatio would budge.
Kill that Jew, men!

A SOLDIER

                                        Heard and done.

ISSA

It is finished!

PUBLIUS

Ill begun
When the Roman virtue sleeps!

AGRIPPA

Death, man! See the tide that sweeps
From his side, a pinkish flood
Of foaming water mixed with blood.
It swells; it washes all the hill —

PUBLIUS

It sweeps out valour, duty, will.
Sordid luxury shall tame
The grand old Roman fame.
Let us go! the filthy spate
Washes out all good within me.
Fear and softness, hurry and hate
Seem to stab me, storm me, win me.
Virtue reels inebriate:
Rome is flung upon her fate.

(He wheels with the rest, as they march down the hill.
Above, a faintly luminous Shadow, appears Alexander the
king, or as it were an image of his image.)

ALEXANDER

The flood sweeps on
From horizon to horizon.
Beauty, strength, virtue, all are gone.

(The eclipse passes.)

Now sudden springs the natural face
Of all the earth's old grace.
The broad sun smiles, as if that fatal close
Of the revel in the garden of Eros

Had never been.
Yet to this keen
Sight, to this sleuth-hound scent for subtle truth,
The essential youth
Of things is all corrupt. I will away
Into the mystic palaces of Pan
Hidden from day,
Hidden from man,
Awaiting there the coming of the Sphinx
Whose genius drinks
The poison of this pestilence, and saves
The world from all its lords and slaves.
Ho! for his chariot-wheels that whirl afar!
His hawk's eye flashing through the silver star!
Upon the heights his standard shall he plant
Free, equal, passionate, pagan, dominant,
Mystic, indomitable, self-controlled,
The red rose glowing on the cross of gold...

Yea! I will wait throughout the centuries
Of the universal man-disease
Until that morn of his Titanic birth...
The Saviour of the Earth!